CAN YOU SEE IT? 2

A JOLLY HOLIDAY ADVENTURE

Troll

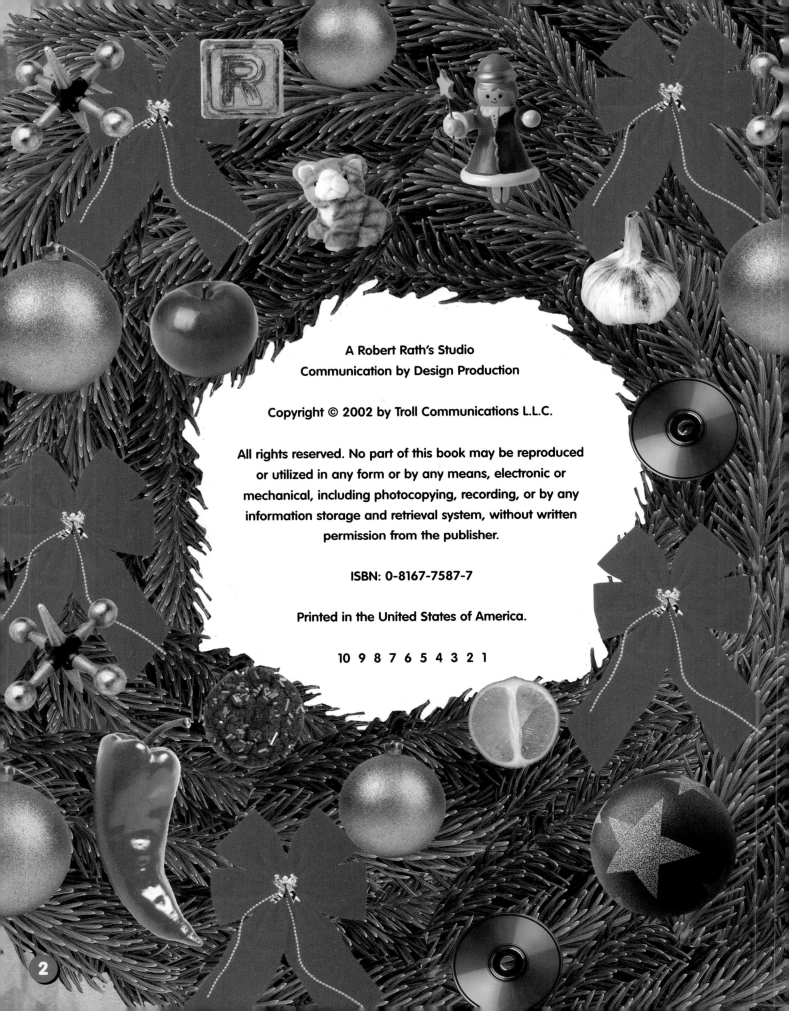

A Robert Rath's Studio
Communication by Design Production

ISBN: 0-8167-7587-7

Printed in the United States of America.

10 9 8 7 6 5 4 3 2 1

CONTENTS

4   Feast Your Eyes!

6   Sounds of the Season

8   Hanukkah Dreidel Hunt

10   Christmas Tree Look-n-See

12   Search the Snow High & Low

14   Unwrap the Unwanted Gifts

16   The 12 Dogs of Christmas

18   Hidden Holiday

20   Kwanzaa Fun Find!

22   Santa's Slackers

24   Snow-Sport Spotting

26   Christmas Eve at the Mall

28   Seek out the Unsweet

30   Holiday Mascots Hide-n-Seek!

Super Search!

As you search this book through and through,
Keep your eyes peeled for these things, too:

eleven baseballs

five fishing lures

three toy farmers

four pizza cutters

two kettles

three sunglasses

Feast Your

Eyes!

Menu

Belly up to this table of treats.
Don't worry — it's pretend.
Have all you can eat!

Can You Find:

five broken eggs
three partly-eaten doughnuts
eight pretzels
one red chili pepper
three cloves of garlic
two bowls of cereal
three jars of pickles
three forks
two waffles
three mushrooms
one scarecrow
three blocks of Swiss cheese

Sounds of the Season

Jingle bells, jingle bells, jingle all the way.
Oh, what fun it is to hide — these bells for you to play.

Can
You
Find:
six Santa bells
one angel-handle bell
four yellow bells
one party horn

three red bells
one 1878 bell
two alarm clocks
one old telephone

one bell decoration
two whistles
one blue bicycle bell

Hanukkah

בֿ
Nun

ג
Gimel

ה
Hay

שׁ
Shin

Nun, Gimel, Hay, Shin —
Around, around the dreidels spin.

Dreidel Hunt

Can You Find:

eight green "shin" letters
twenty gold coins
five dark blue dreidels
six white "hay" letters

one orange dreidel
nine blue "nun" letters
four gold "gimel" letters

**These dreidels you see aren't made of clay,
but you can play with them anyway.**

Christmas Tree Look-n-See

We've decorated the tree —
it's finally done.
Don't be a Scrooge —
let's have some fun!

Can You Find:

two drums
seven cookies
seven Santas
three snowflakes
three medals
three burned-out lights
one queen of Egypt
one polar bear
eight angels
two horses

Snowmen abound
in this forest of fun.
If you find all ten,
well then, you've won!

SEARCH THE SNOW!

HIGH & LOW

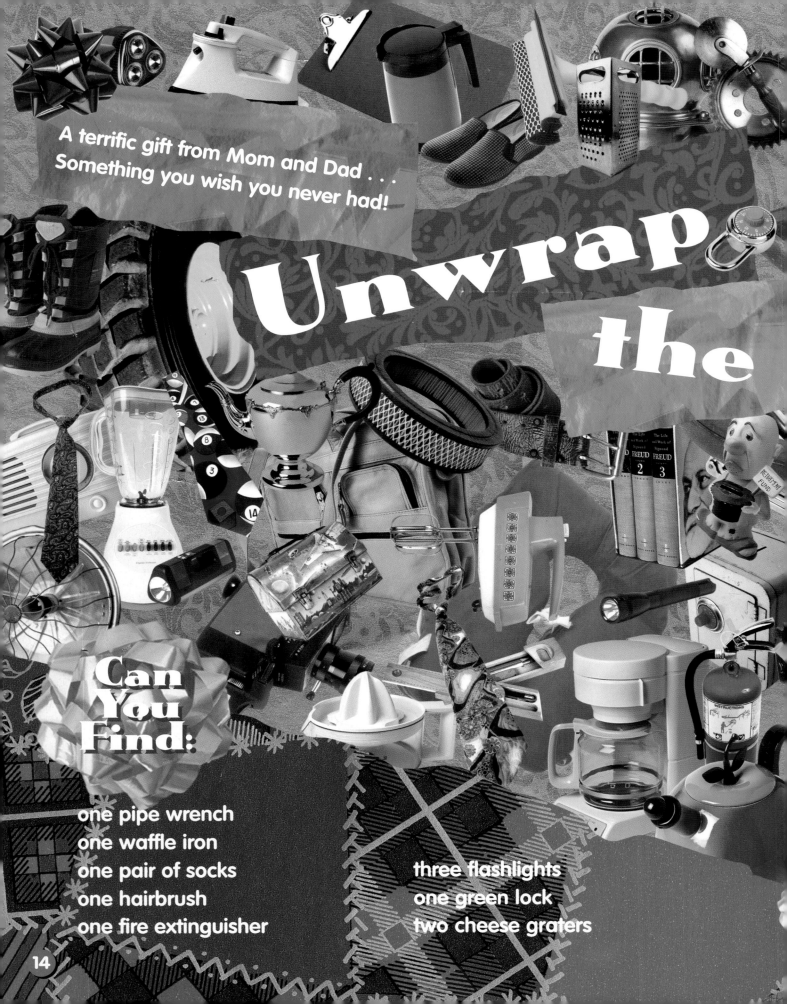

A terrific gift from Mom and Dad . . .
Something you wish you never had!

Unwrap the

Can You Find:

one pipe wrench
one waffle iron
one pair of socks
one hairbrush
one fire extinguisher

three flashlights
one green lock
two cheese graters

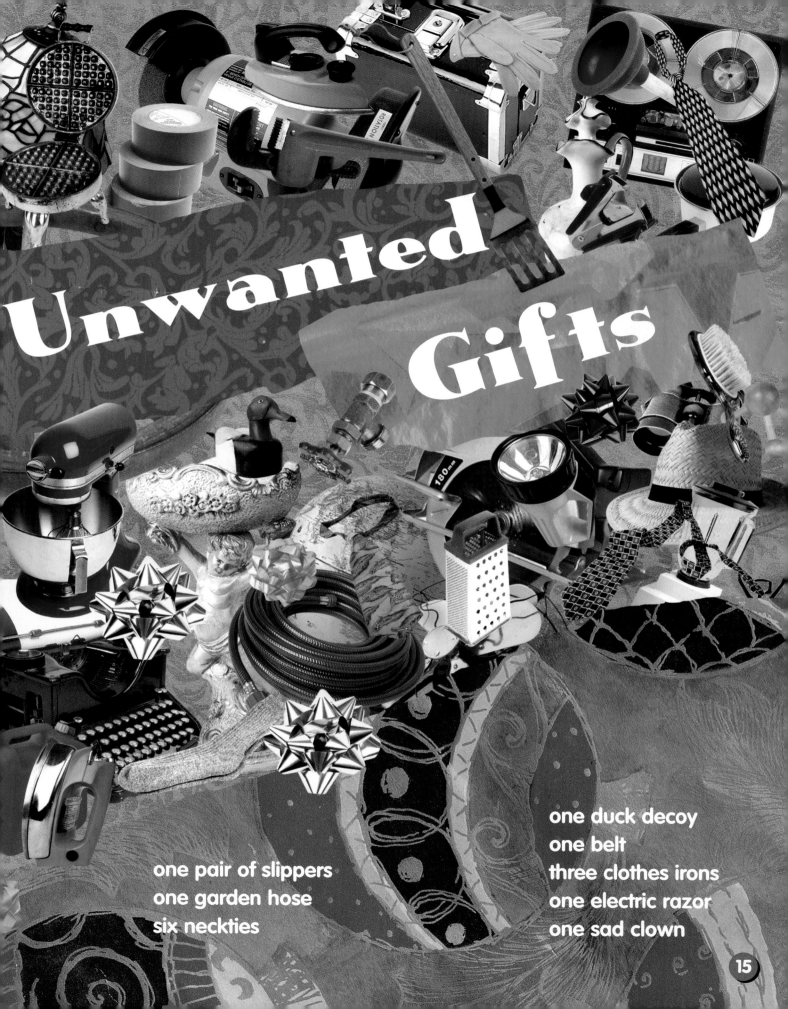

Unwanted Gifts

one pair of slippers
one garden hose
six neckties

one duck decoy
one belt
three clothes irons
one electric razor
one sad clown

On the twelfth day of Christmas, my true love gave to me:

The 12 Dogs of Christmas

Try this version
of the classic song.
"Paws" for a moment,
and then bark along!

As you sing with
all your might,
Find all the doggies
within your sight.

two St. Bernards, and a bulldog scratching a flea.

three bloodhounds,

four collie dogs,

five—Great—Danes,

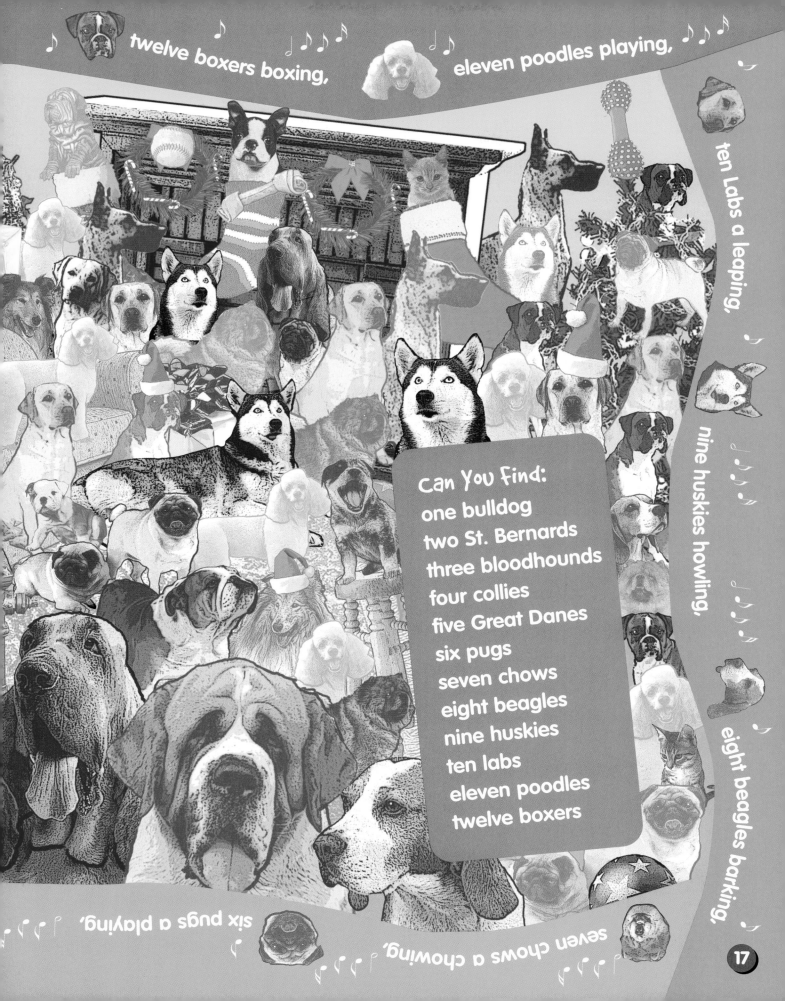

twelve boxers boxing, eleven poodles playing,

ten Labs a leaping, nine huskies howling, eight beagles barking,

Can You Find:
one bulldog
two St. Bernards
three bloodhounds
four collies
five Great Danes
six pugs
seven chows
eight beagles
nine huskies
ten labs
eleven poodles
twelve boxers

six pugs a playing, seven chows a chowing,

HIDDEN HOLIDAY

In this mixed-up
letter maze,
Find letters to spell
"HAPPY HOLIDAYS."

Once you've found
this phrase with ease,
Look for other letter
shapes if you please!

CAN YOU FIND:

three T shapes
five C shapes
five E shapes
five W shapes
two V shapes
one shape
for each letter
of the alphabet

With unity, family, and community its mission —
Kwanzaa celebrates African culture and tradition.
The special colors of Kwanzaa are black, red, and green.
So look for colorful critters in this African scene.

KWANZAA

CAN YOU FIND:

 two blue fish

 one orange warthog

 five purple wildebeasts

 three blue mice

 five gold frogs

 seven orange ants

 two green turtles

 three orange lions

three yellow bees

one brown camel

two green snakes

FUN FIND!

SANTA'S SLACKERS

Santa is busy preparing his sleigh, while inside the workshop, his elves are at play!

CAN YOU FIND THESE ELVES:

one on a rocking horse
one on a bike
two in dump trucks
one napping
one in a baby stroller
one playing basketball
one fishing
two playing baseball
one juggling blocks
one playing with puppets
four riding in cars
one playing guitar

Sporting Spot—Sports=News

This snowboarding dude is catching some air.
Find all the sport stuff — even look in his hair.

six ice skate snowflakes
one old snowshoe
three wool sock snowflakes
two hockey masks
four ski boot snowflakes

Can You Find:

one wooden toboggan
two compasses
three pairs of skis
two red ski boots
three winter hats

Seek Out the Unsweet

Among mouthwatering chocolates and sweet candy swirls, what puckers your mouth or makes your toes curl?

Can You Find:

- six carrots
- three broccoli pieces
- one red onion
- four cauliflower heads
- one pink grapefruit slice
- five artichokes
- one lime slice
- three red peppers
- one mushroom
- two radishes
- two lemon slices
- three pea pods

Holiday Mascots Hide-n-Seek!

Though these pages are filled
with old Christmas cheer,
you must search for symbols
of other holidays dear.

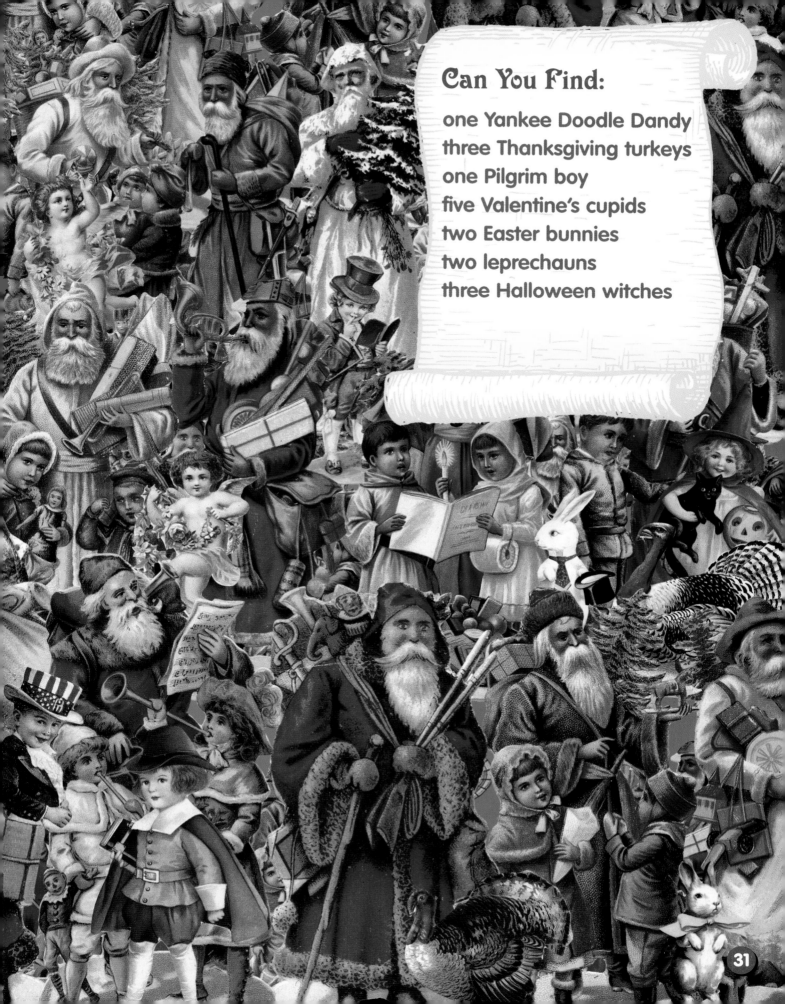

Can You Find:

one Yankee Doodle Dandy
three Thanksgiving turkeys
one Pilgrim boy
five Valentine's cupids
two Easter bunnies
two leprechauns
three Halloween witches

If you think you've finished the book,
Go back and take another look!

Can You Find:

one Viking helmet   one bottle of milk

one hedgehog   one clipboard

To Kathy and Lucy, for finding me. — R.R.

For Edualdo the magnificent and
Kaiya the "howling husky." — P.R.